TIM JEFFS ART
—Animal Sketches—

European Wildlife

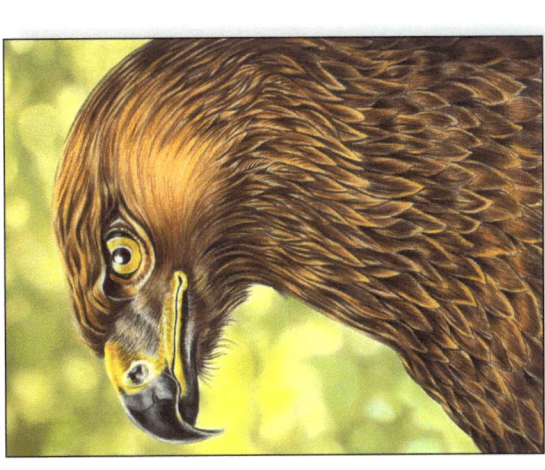

ANIMALS OF THE WORLD Coloring Book Series

For Jane, Jenna and Harrison

Dedicated to all of the wonderful colorists who have supported my art and made my drawings more beautiful with their colors, and all the precious creatures that we live among.

A special thank you to Jo Warren for all of her continued support and beautiful colorings and lesson that make this book so much more special, and Karl Jennings for all of his continued support.

Grayscale coloring page before...

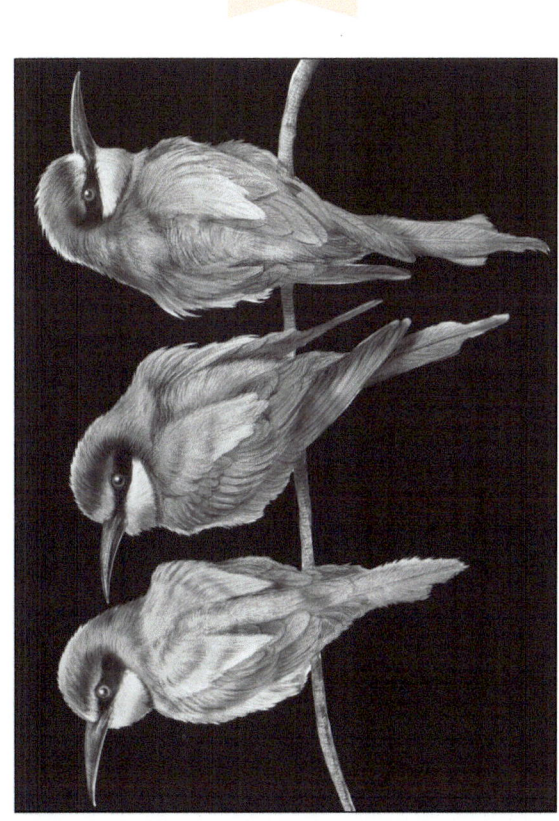

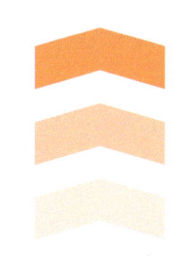

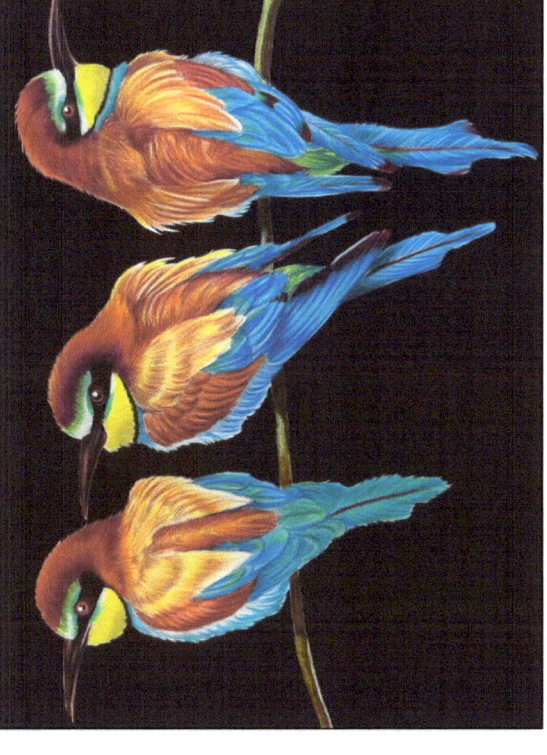

...and after you bring it to life with your colorful imagination!

© Copyright 2022 Tim Jeffs Art

All rights reserved. No part of this publication may be reproduced or distributed in any form without the prior written permission of Tim Jeffs Art.

Tim Jeffs Art

376 East Madison Avenue, Dumont, NJ 07628

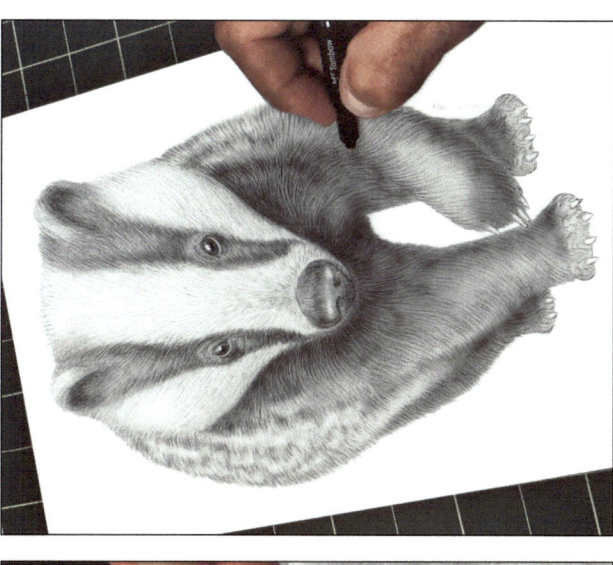
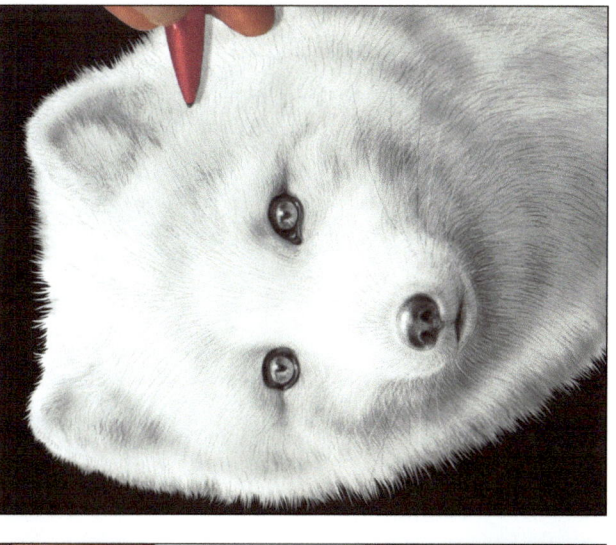
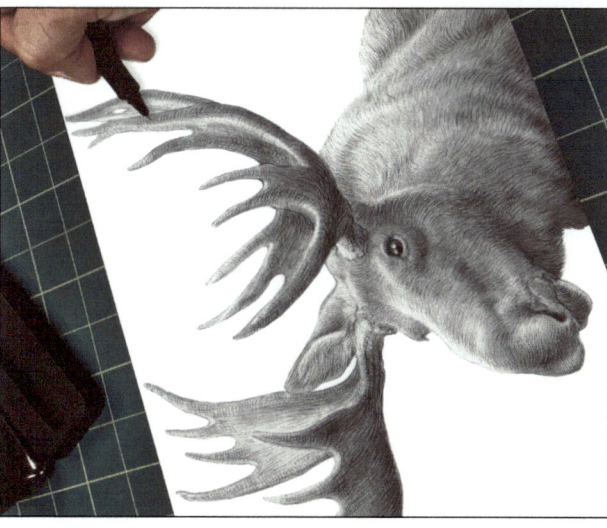

Drawing European Wildlife

Lucky Seventh! Though this series of coloring books wasn't published in any particular order, this book is the last book of seven continents that I have covered in my *Animals of the World Coloring Book* series. It has been such a wonderful journey learning about and drawing the many different creatures that live all over our planet.

Europe is sometimes called a subcontinent of Eurasia. But by no means is it small. It covers almost 4 million square miles. Many animal species have been introduced into Europe, but for this book I choose to draw Europe's native species including the European Bison, Iberian Lynx, Polar Bear, Moose, European Bee-eater, and Golden Eagle.

I hope you enjoy coloring this group of European Wildlife sketches as much as I enjoyed drawing them, and I know that with your colors, you will bring these amazing creatures of the world's second smallest continent to life!

GRAYSCALE COLORING LESSON

Iberian Lynx

Lesson level: Easy

Coloring the
Iberian Lynx

On the next page I will walk you through the coloring of the Iberian Lynx which is on page 8 of this coloring book. This beautiful wild cat was on the verge of extinction with only 94 individuals left in the wild in 2002. With conservation efforts the population has increased to 1011 in 2021. Coloring and sharing your coloring page is a way to continue to spread the word that these animals need our help. I hope you enjoy coloring this spectacular creature as much as I had creating the drawing!

▶ Supply List

In this lesson, Faber Castell Polychromos pencils were used (pencil numbers are listed) but you can use any brand with similar colors.

1) **The coloring page can be found on page 8**
2) **Faber Castell Polychromos Pencils:**

103 Ivory
187 Burnt Ochre
180 Raw Umber
280 Burnt Umber
199 Black

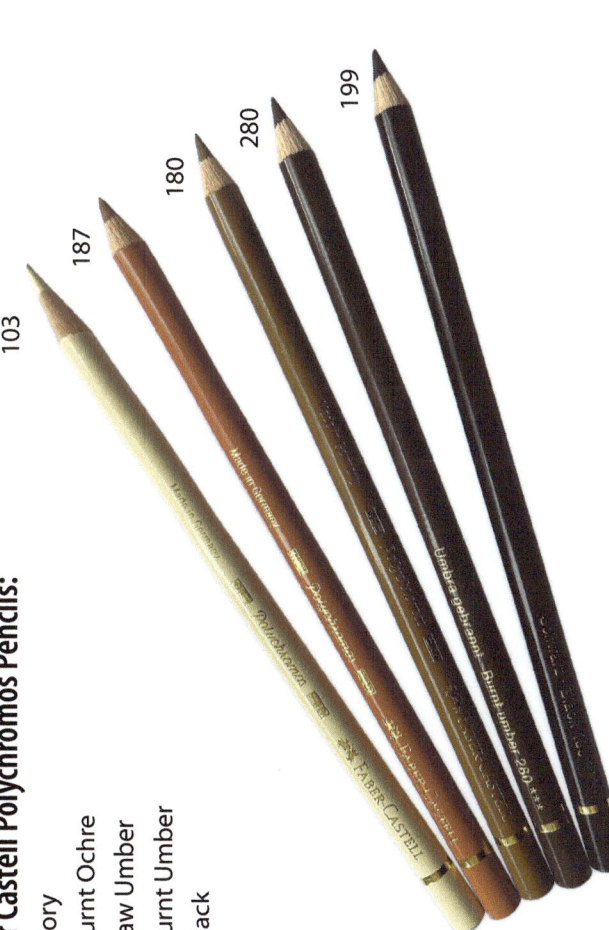

GRAYSCALE COLORING LESSON

Iberian Lynx

Iberian Lynx

Making your Iberian Lynx come to life with color

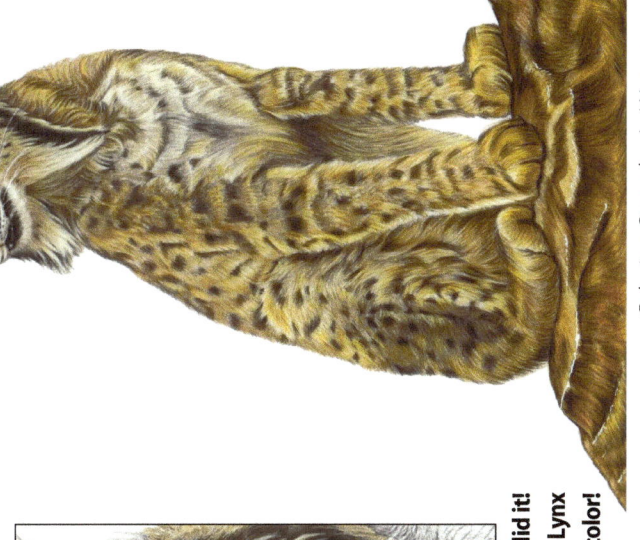

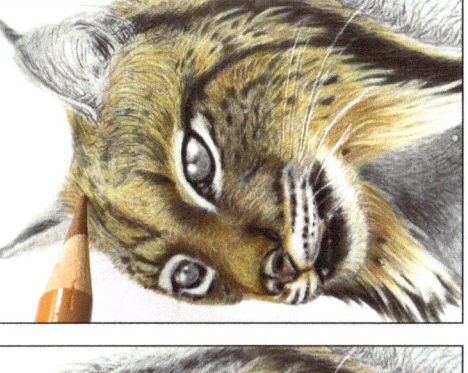
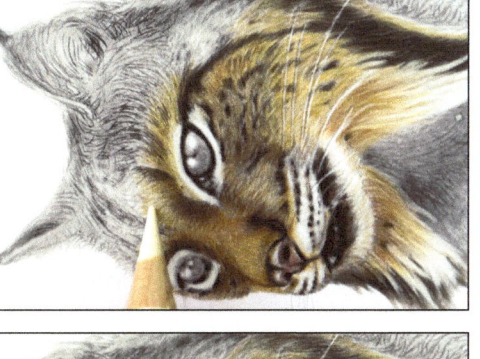
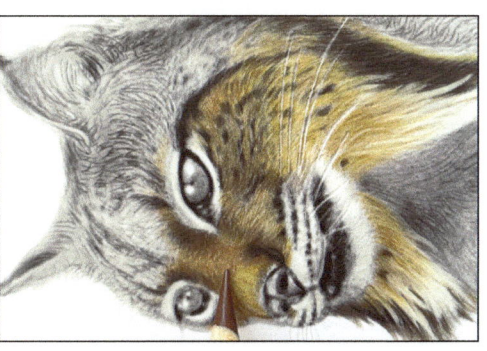
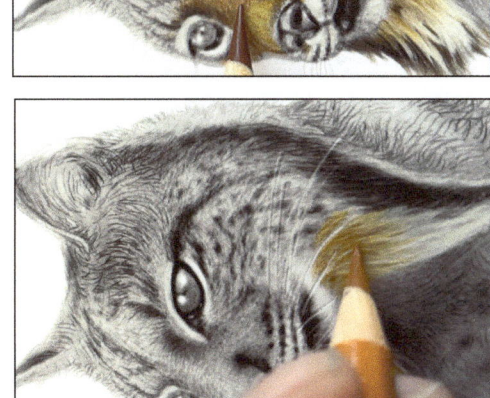

Step 1-4. Start by laying down a base color of Burnt Ochre (187). Leave the ends of the mane, chin, muzzle, and around the eyes free of color. Next create darker fur on the nose by layering Burnt Umber (280) over the base coat. Using Ivory (103) color in the ends of the mane, chin, muzzle, around the eyes, and eye brow. Color the spots, mouth, stripe along the mane, and around the eyes with Black (199). Finally color the forehead and ears using the same technique.

You did it!
Your Iberian Lynx has come to life with color!

Coloring Steps by Jo Warren

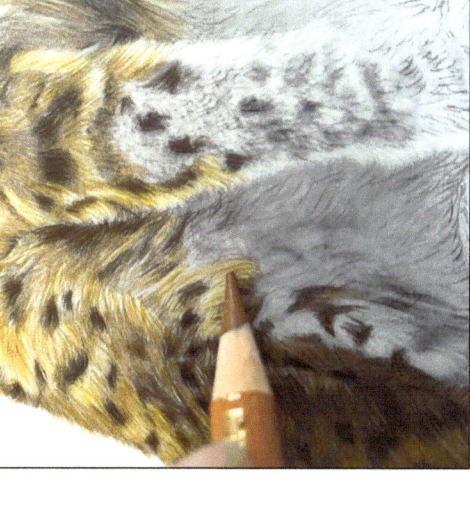

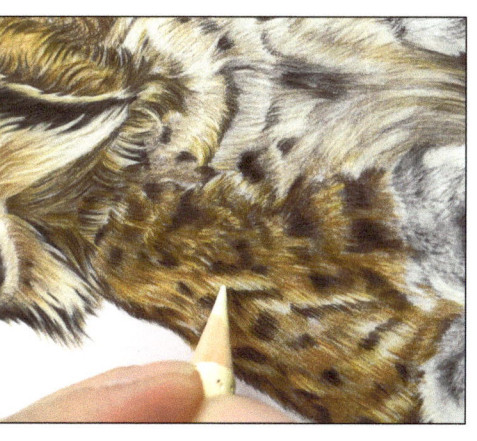

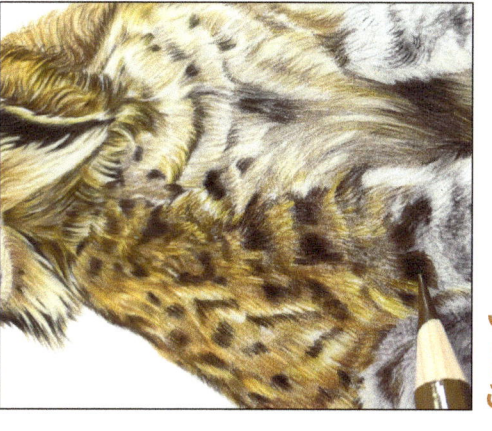

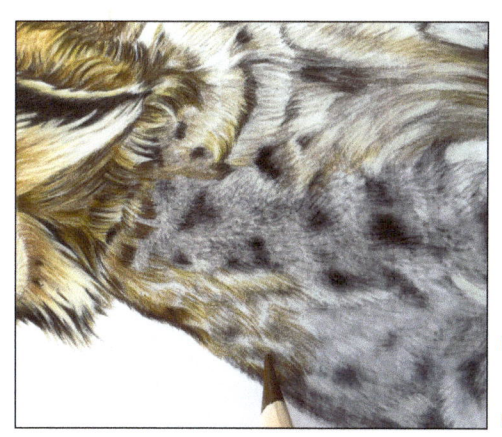

Step 5. Let's try working with a different order of pencils on the back than were used on the head. Following the direction that the fur is flowing make strokes using Burnt Umber (280).

Step 6. Color over the base layer of Burnt Umber with a layer of Burnt Ochre (187). Blend the colors together as you work. Increase the darkness by using Raw Umber (180) on the spots.

Step 7. Next blend the colors together using Ivory (103). **TIP:** The key to making your fur look thick and soft is coloring in the same direction as the hairs are flowing.

Step 8. Continue using the same techniques throughout the body and on the front and back legs. The more time you take to make individual strokes using the four different pencils the more your fur will appear realistic.

Spreading Awareness Through Coloring

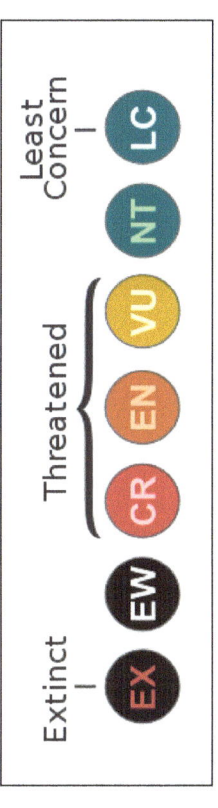

The list consists of 7 categories. From Least Concerned all the way to Extinct. Here are the definitions of each category:

- **LEAST CONCERN (LC):** A species that has been evaluated but not qualified for any other category on the list.
- **NEAR THREATENED (NT):** A species that may be considered threatened with extinction in the near future.
- **VULNERABLE (VU):** A species likely to become endangered unless the circumstances that are threatening its survival and reproduction improve.
- **ENDANGERED (EN):** A species that is considered very likely to become extinct.
- **CRITICALLY ENDANGERED (CR):** A species that is facing an extremely high risk of becoming extinct in the wild.
- **EXTINCT IN THE WILD (EW):** A species that is only known by living members kept in captivity or as a naturalized population outside its historic range due to massive habitat loss.
- **EXTINCT (EX):** A species that has been terminated.

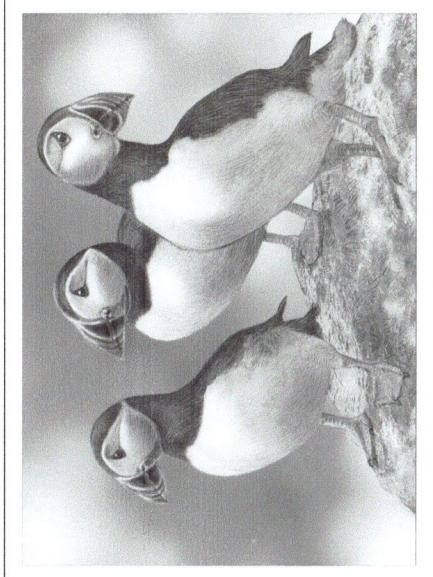

 Atlantic Puffins
Vulnerable

I truly believe that raising awareness through the sharing of my artwork is a fantastic way to educate people about conservation. And coloring animals is a beautiful way to learn about them as you enjoy a relaxing and fun pastime. On the following page, I listed the animals in this book statuses on the *International Union for Conservation of Nature's (IUCN)* conservation list. I think it's important to include the *(IUCN)* conservation list in my books so people understand the classifications more clearly. To the right is an overview of the IUCN's conservation list, which breaks animals' conservation statuses into several categories. Knowing what these categories mean and the animals that are included in them is extremely important. **Together through art we can change the world!**

Tim Jeffs
Animal Artist

Learn About European Wildlife

Before you start coloring, it's important to learn about the animals in this book and their conservation status. And after you finish a coloring share your work on social media to help raise awareness about the animals conservation status.

▶ Arctic Fox Also known as the White Fox and Polar Fox they are found in the Northern Arctic regions and live in some of the most frigid extremes on Earth. They can grow up to 27 inches in length. **Conservation Status:** Least Concern

▶ Atlantic Puffins Found in the North Atlantic Ocean, Northwest Europe, and parts of the Arctic. 90% of the population is found in Europe. Pollution and Climate Change have affected their populations. **Conservation Status:** Vulnerable

▶ European Bee-Eaters A richly colored bird they live in Southern and Central Europe and migrate to Northern and Southern Africa. They feed on bees, wasps and hornets and can eat around 250 bees a day. **Conservation Status:** Least Concern

▶ European Bison They are the heaviest land animal in Europe. During the middle ages they became extinct in the wild in Europe. Now through captive breeding several thousand have been returned to the wild in Europe. **Conservation Status:** Near Threatened

▶ European Badger Native to most of Europe this powerfully built animal grows up to 35 inches in length and has short and strong legs and long claws. Their population is healthy. **Conservation Status:** Least Concern

▶ European Green Lizard It can be found across Southeastern Europe. It's a large lizard growing up to 6 inches in length and the males have a bluish throat. **Conservation Status:** Least Concern

▶ Golden Eagle A large raptor with a wingspan of up to 7 feet it is found throughout Eurasia and in parts of North America and North Africa. Their population is strong at around 250,000. **Conservation Status:** Least Concern

▶ Iberian Lynx Found only on the Iberian Peninsula in Southwestern Europe they are threatened due to over-hunting and poaching. Their numbers have been increasing in the wild from only 94 in 2002, to 1011 in 2021. **Conservation Status:** Endangered

▶ Moose Found in large numbers across Eurasia they are the largest and heaviest extant species of the deer family. Adult males can reach 7 feet tall and weigh up to 1500 pounds. Their populations are relatively stable. **Conservation Status:** Least Concern

▶ Peacock Butterfly Also known as the European Peacock this colorful butterfly is found in woods, meadows and parks throughout Europe and Asia. They have two large eye spots on their wings that are thought to be an anti-predator mechanism. **Conservation Status:** Least Concern

▶ Pine Marten Also known as the European Pine Marten they inhabit well-wooded areas of Europe, Russia and parts of the Middle East. They have light to dark brown fur and grow up to 10 inches long. **Conservation Status:** Least Concern

▶ Polar Bear The largest extant bear species their range is largely within the Arctic Circle and Arctic Ocean. Males can grow up to 1500 pounds. Their population is threatened due to habitat loss and climate change. **Conservation Status:** Vulnerable

▶ Red Deer Found in the United Kingdom, throughout Europe, Southwestern Asia and North Africa. They are one of the largest species of deer and weigh up to 500lbs and 7.5 feet tall. **Conservation Status:** Least Concern

▶ Wolf The global wolf population is around 300,000 and considered stable. They are native to Eurasia and North America. Wolves are social animals and live in packs. **Conservation Status:** Least Concern

▶ Wolverine They are found in mainland Nordic countries of Europe and throughout Russia and Siberia. They have ferocity and strength and are equipped with crampon-like large claws. They are widely distributed and their population is strong. **Conservation Status:** Least Concern

European Wildlife Index

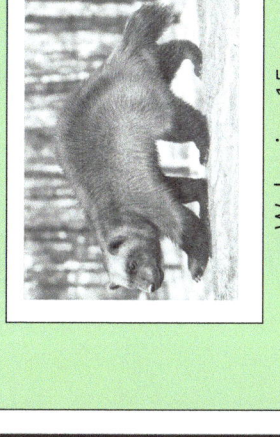
Red Deer 13

Wolf 14

Wolverine 15

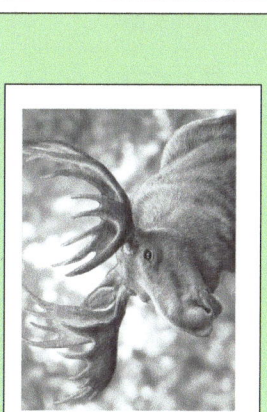
Peacock Butterfly 10

Pine Marten 11

Polar Bear 12

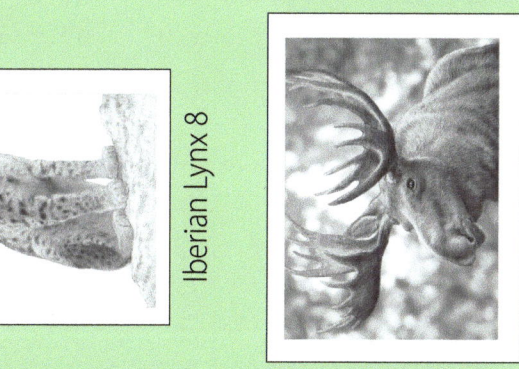
Golden Eagle 7

Iberian Lynx 8

Moose 9

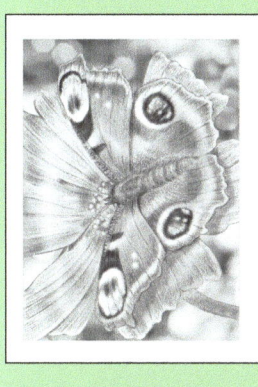
European Bison 4

European Badger 5

European Green Lizard 6

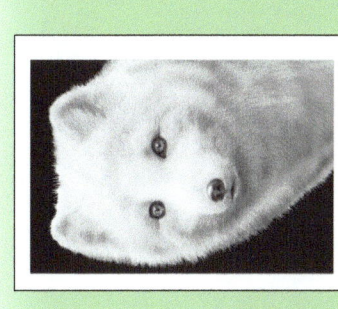
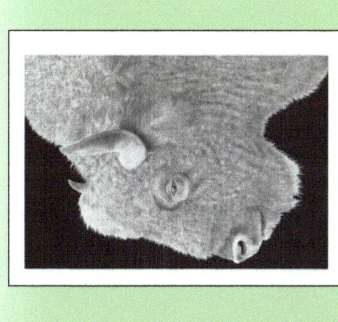
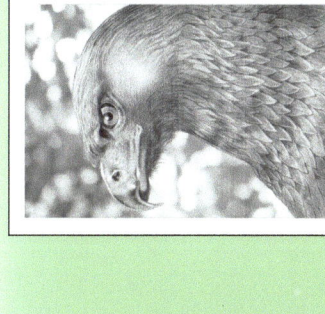
Arctic Fox 1

Atlantic Puffins 2

European Bee-Eaters 3

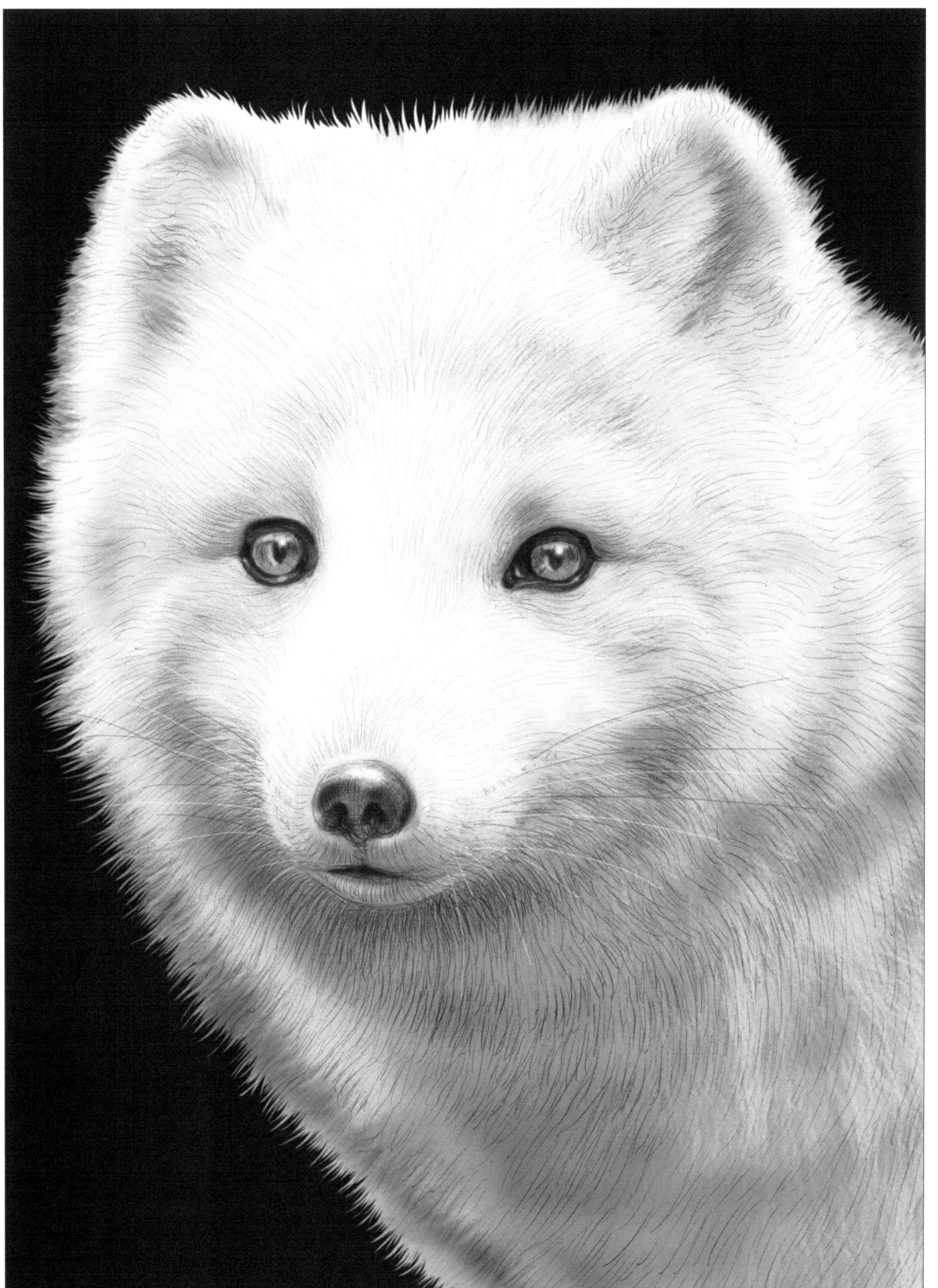

Arctic Fox

Atlantic Puffins

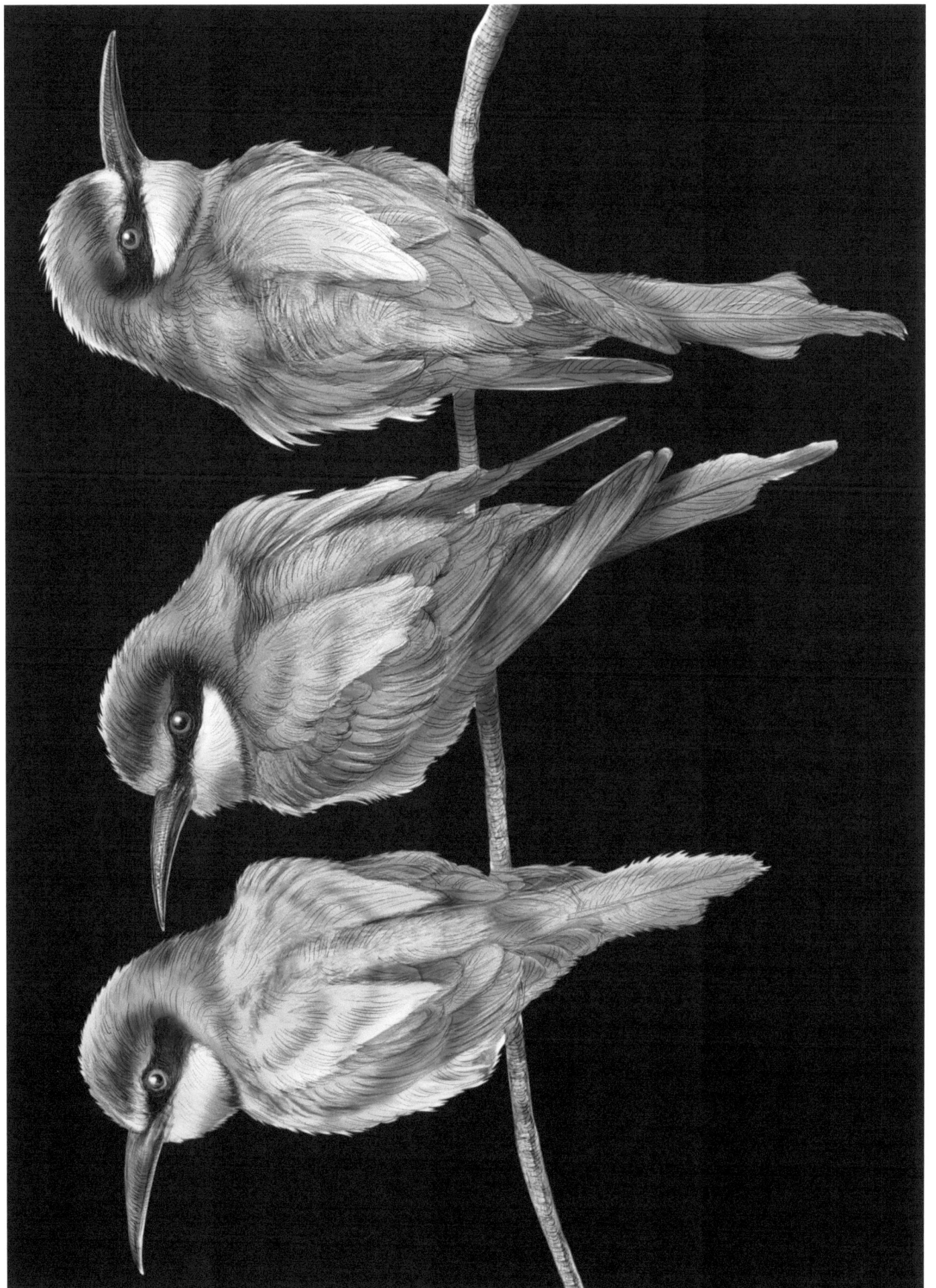

European Bee-Eaters

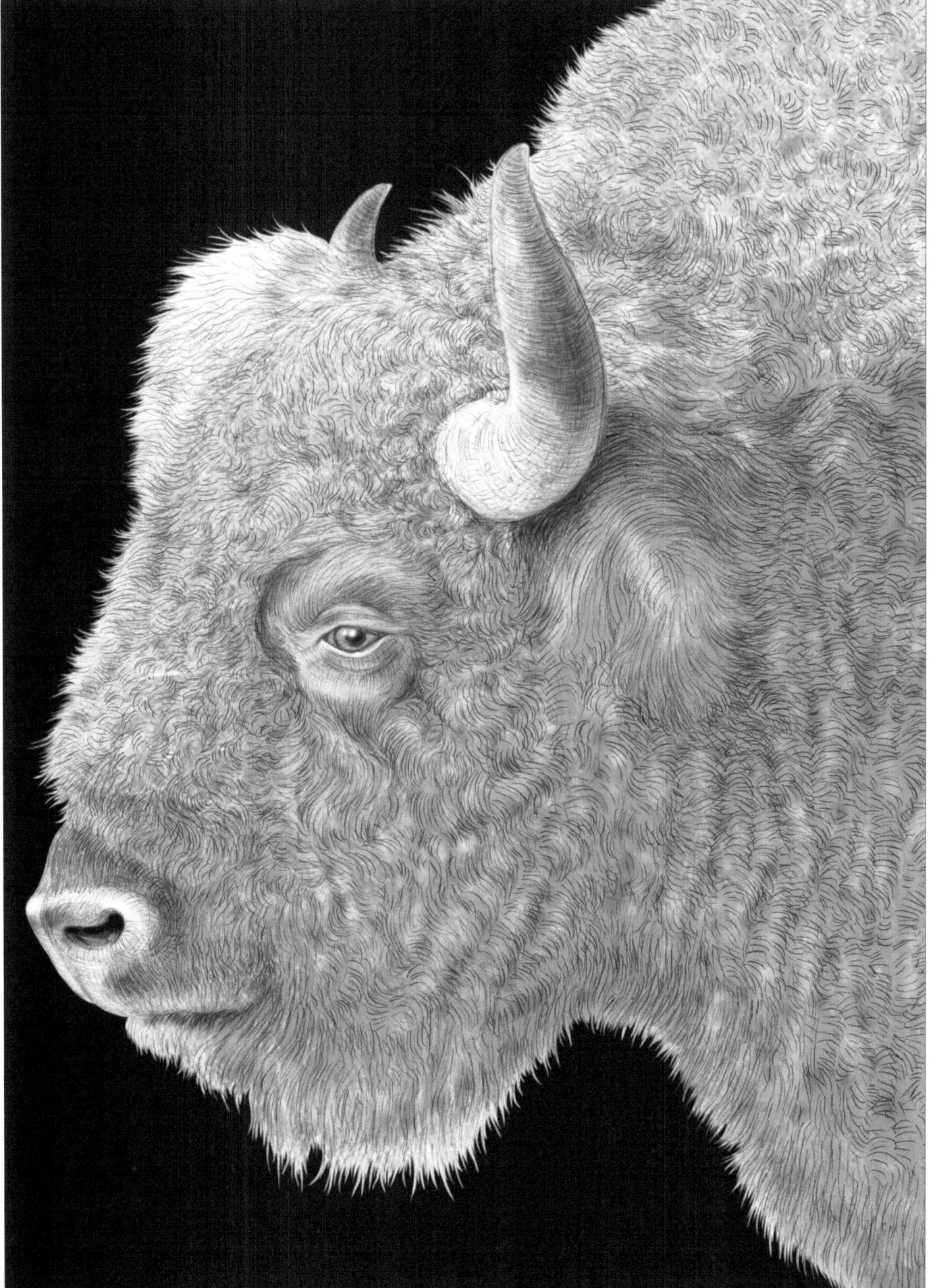

European Bison

European Badger

European Green Lizard

Golden Eagle

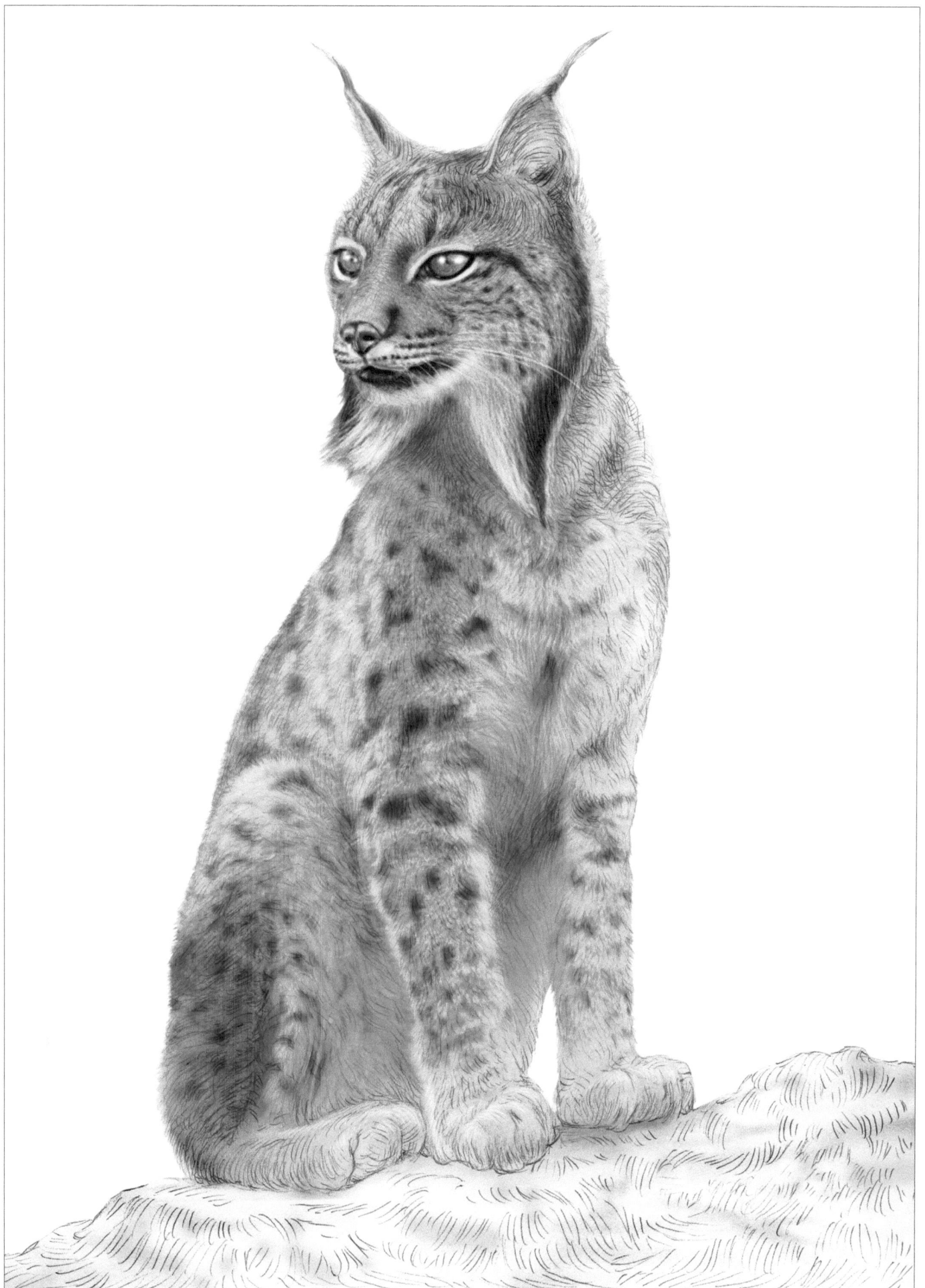

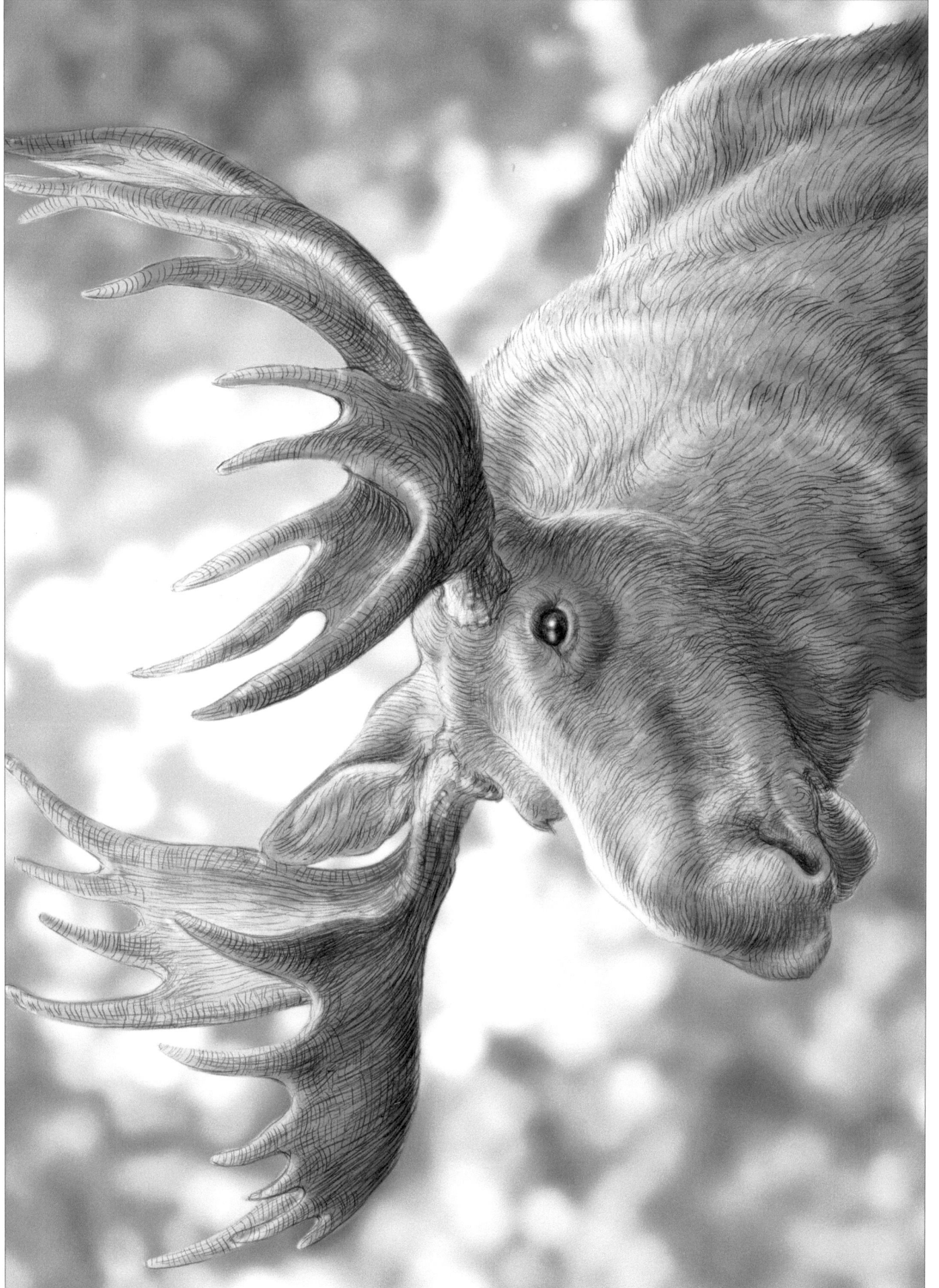

Moose

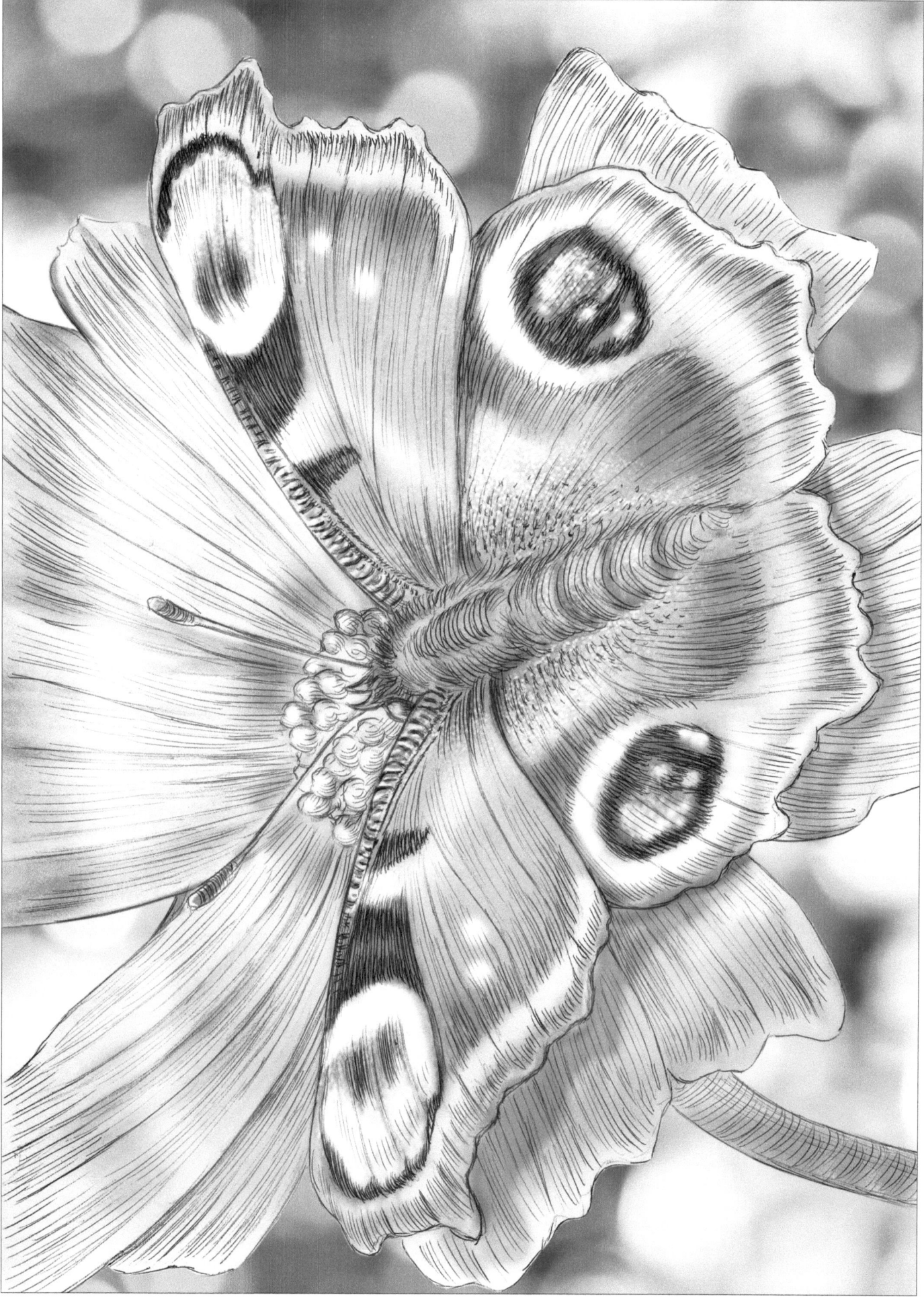

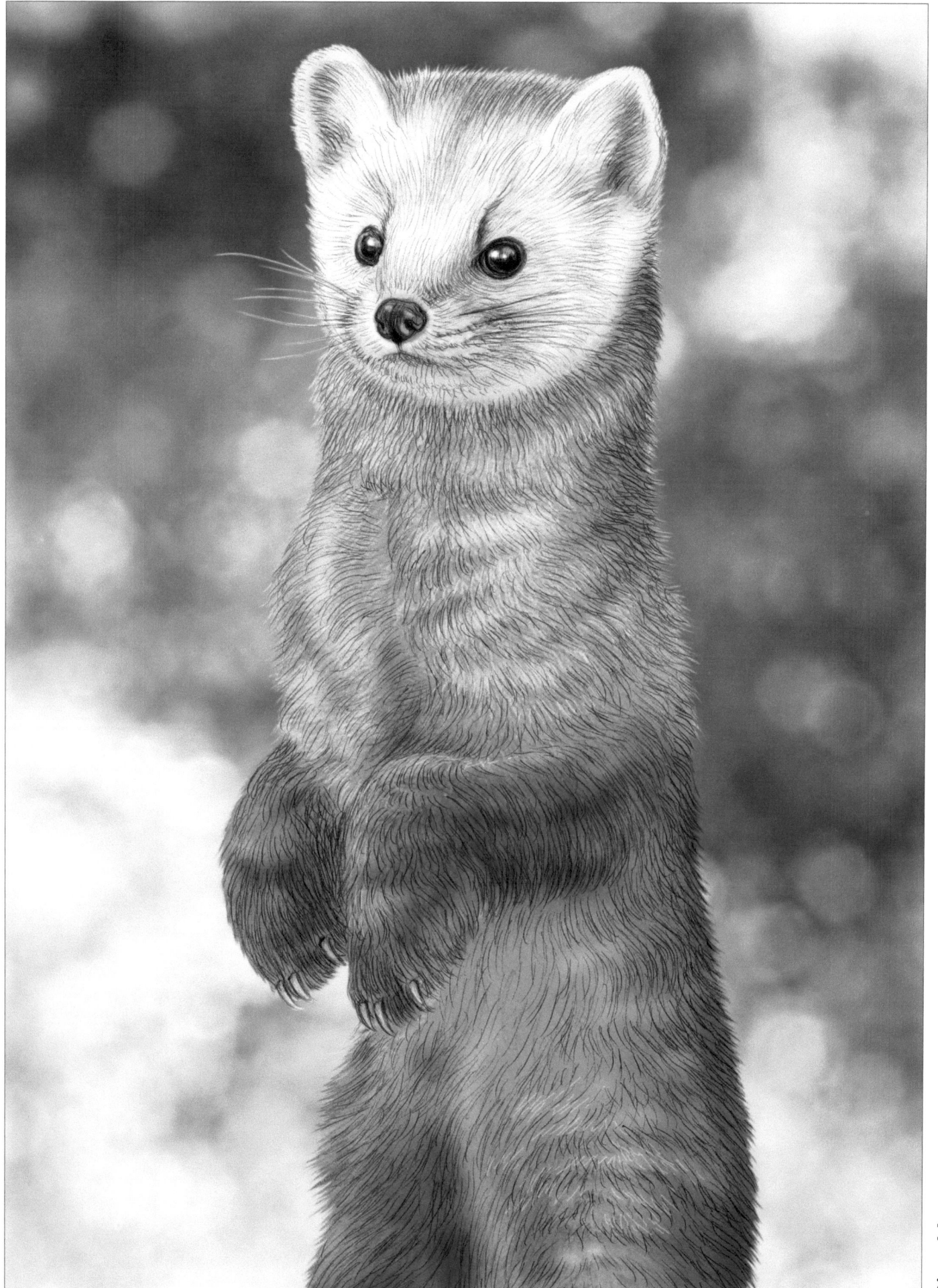

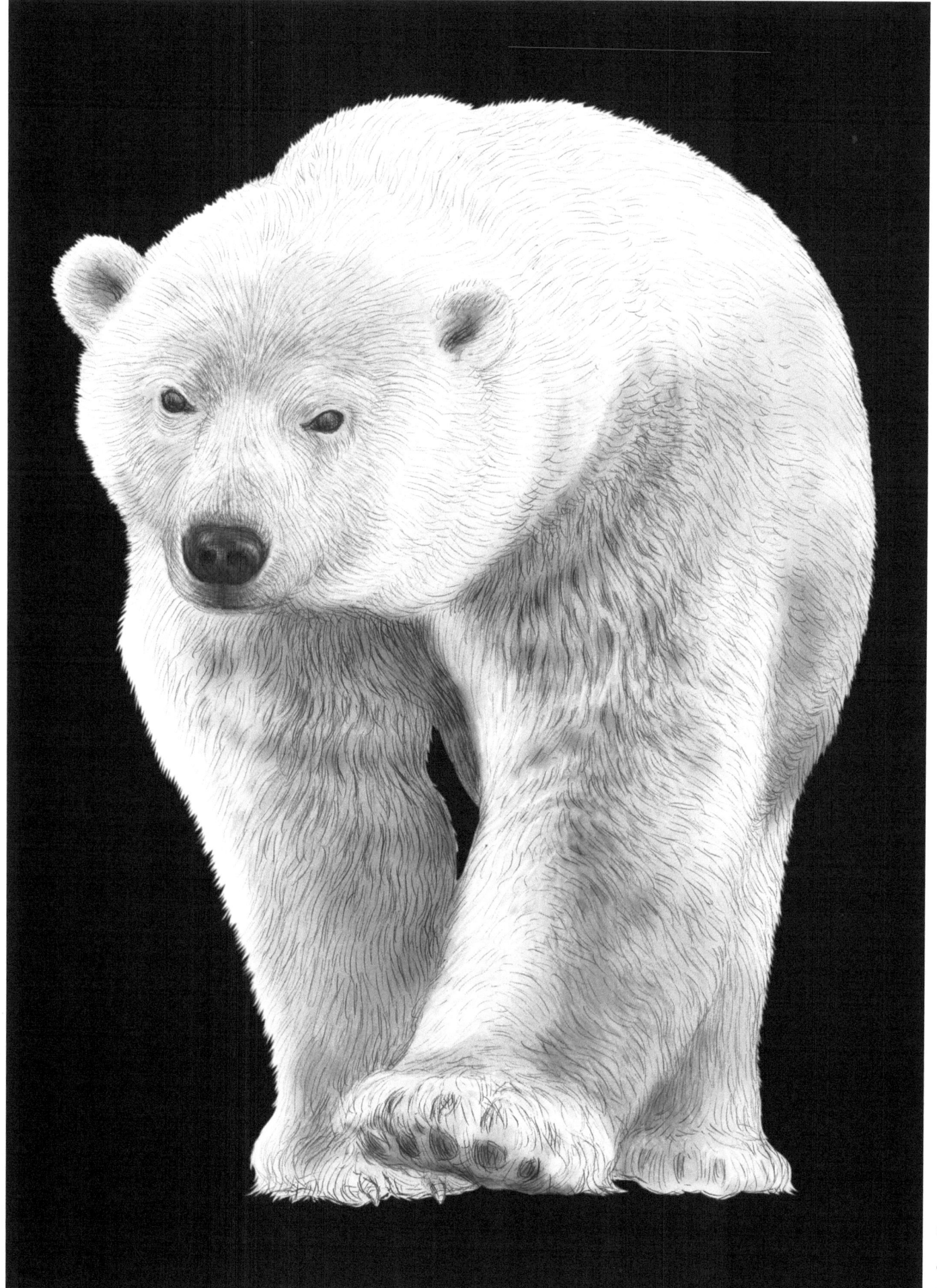

Polar Bear

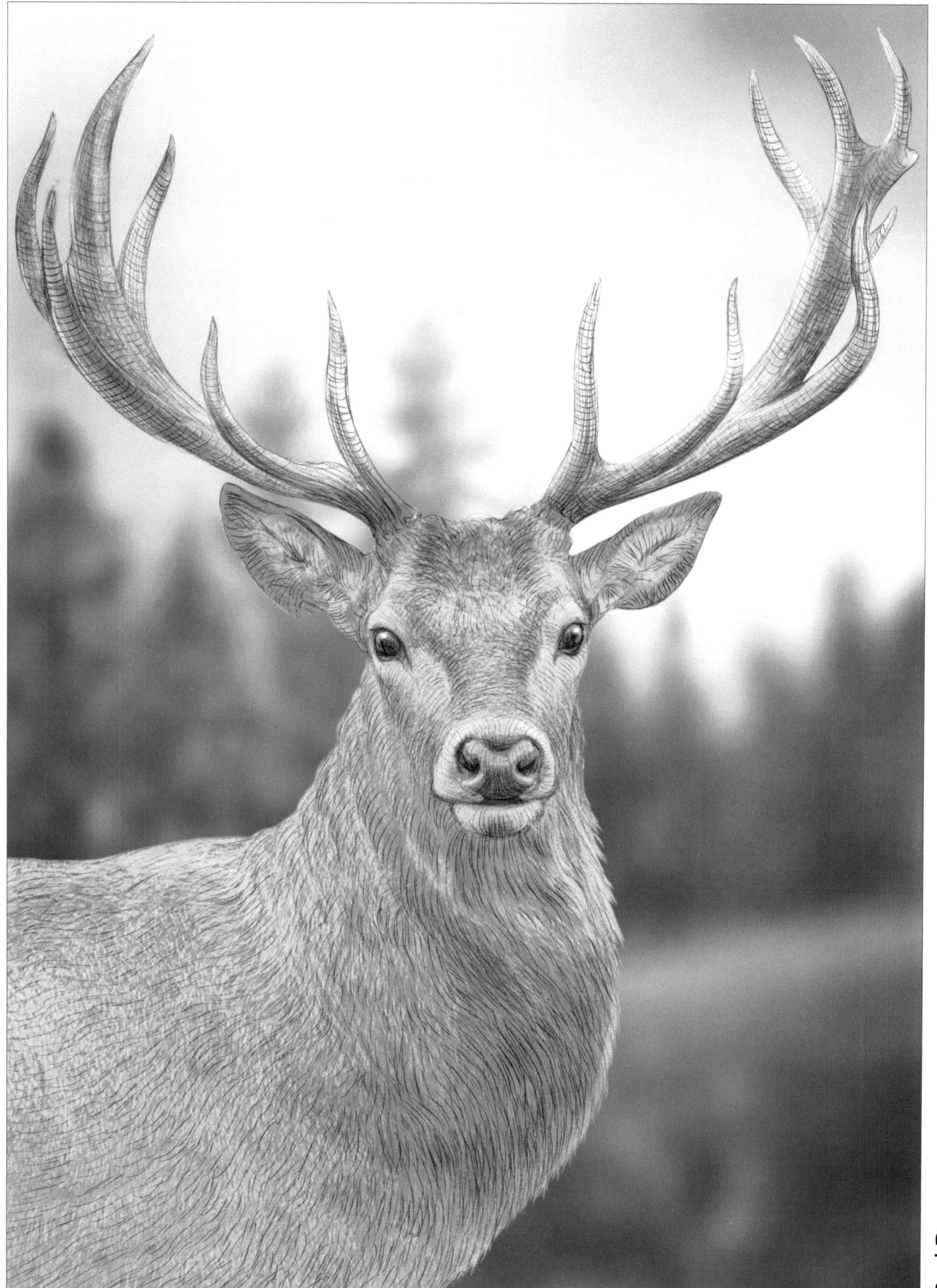

Red Deer

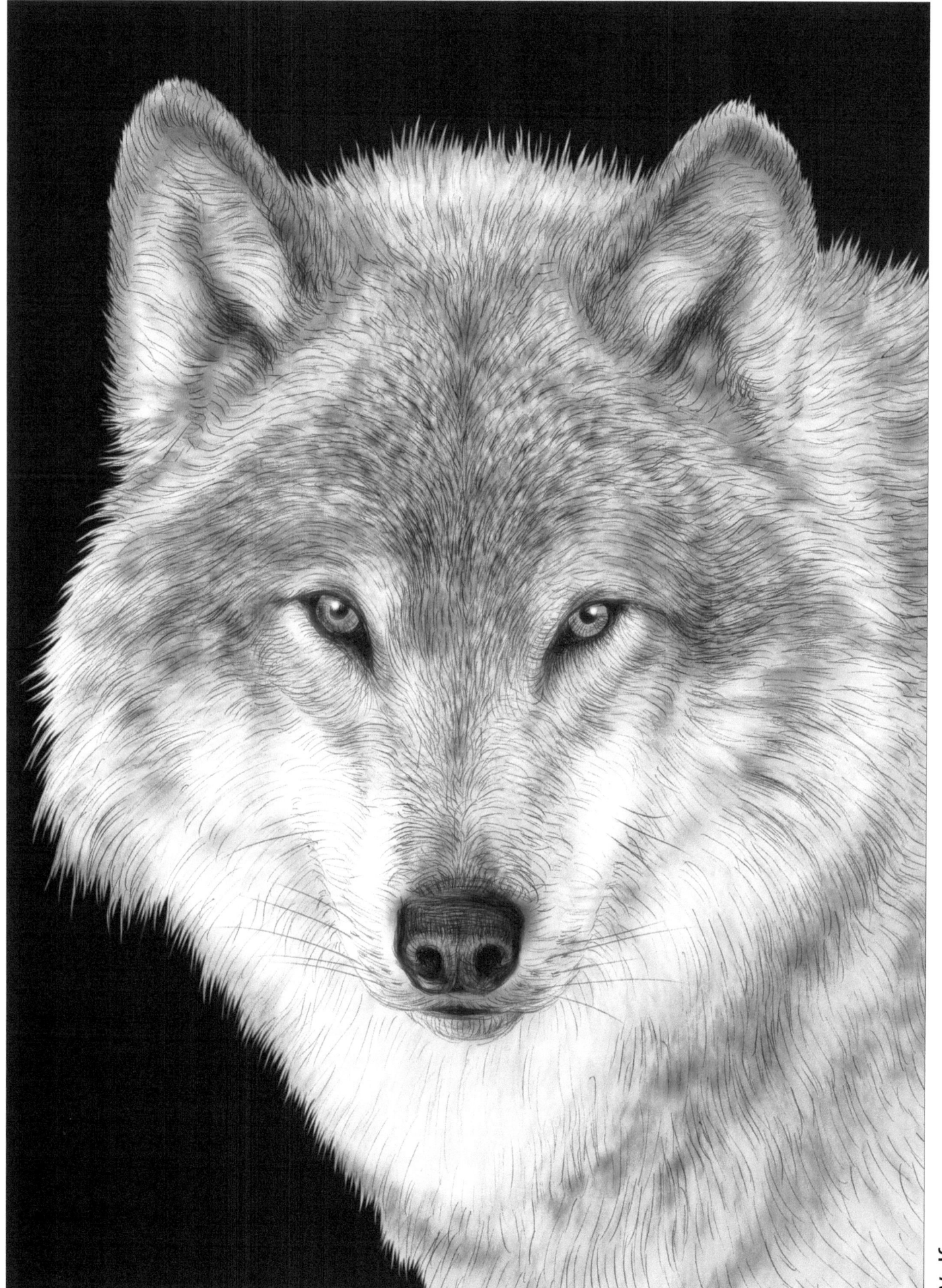

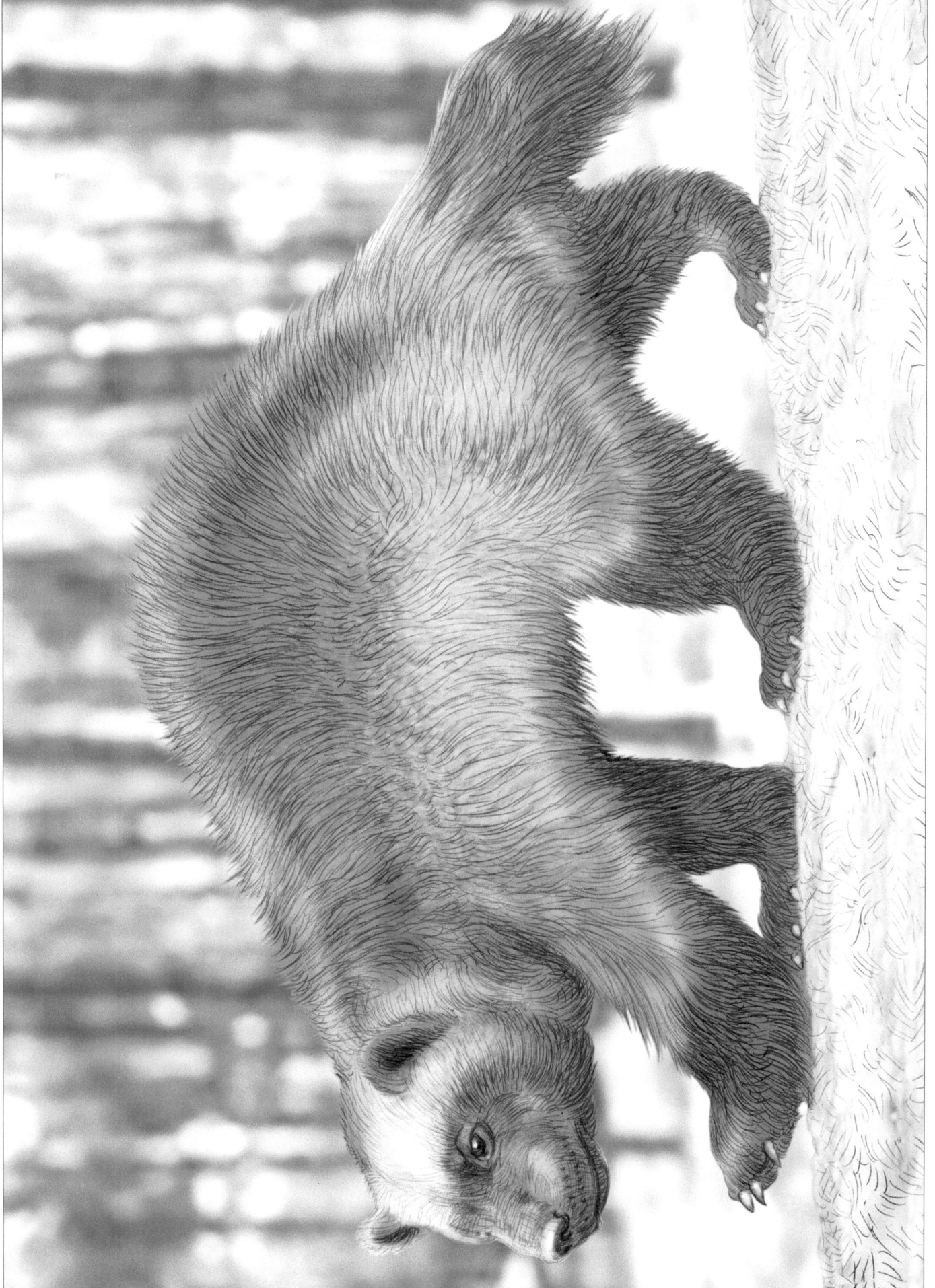

Wolverine

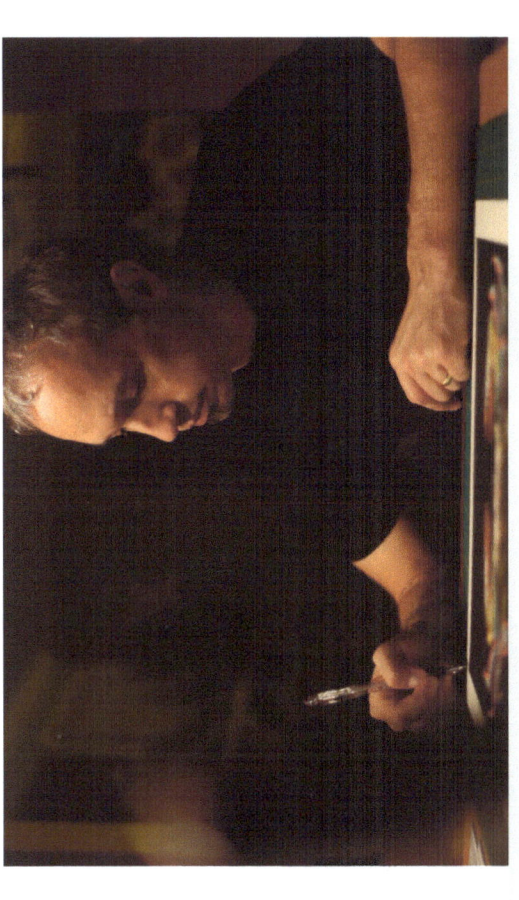

Tim Jeffs is a New York City based artist and illustrator who has been creating dynamic artwork for over 25 years. Animals are a favorite subject matter of his, along with the complex and intricate details these creatures possess. *"The incredible diversity and complexity of animals has always intrigued me. They offer endless pleasure to look and marvel upon. In every drawing I try to capture the unique quality of each particular animal. I hope you enjoy my perspective, love and admiration of these incredible creatures."*

Visit my website for prints, digital coloring books and coloring lessons:

www.TimJeffsArt.com

Discover the full line of Tim Jeffs' Published Coloring Books

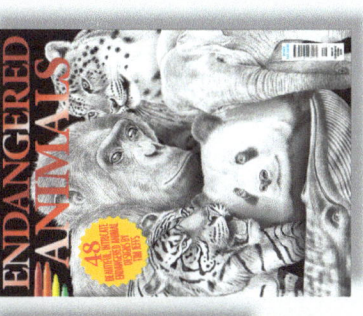

**Colouring Heaven Collection
Endangered Animals**
Available at: Colouringheaven.com

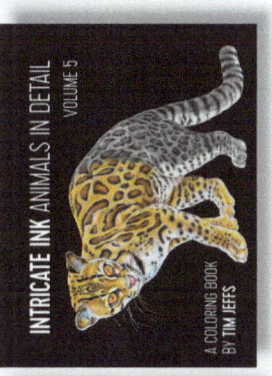
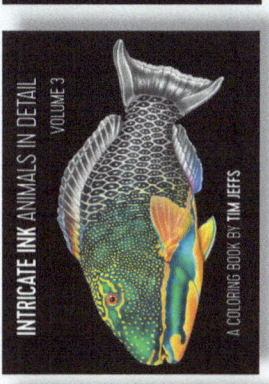
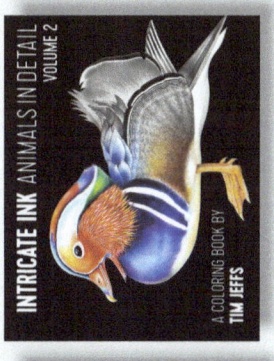

Intricate Ink Animals In Detail Volume 1, 2 3 and 5, and Intricate Animal Drawings Volume 1 and 2 are available at:
Amazon.com
Bookdepository.com

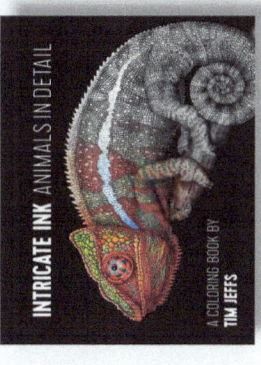

Discover Tim Jeffs' Merchandise

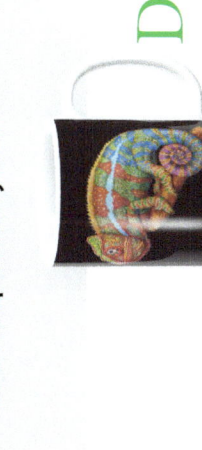

Etsy Shop
www.etsy.com/shop/TimJeffsArt

Society6 Shop
www.society6.com/TimJeffsArt

Redbubble Shop
TimJeffsArt.redbubble.com

TeePublic Shop
https://www.teepublic.com/user/tim-jeffs-art

Discover the full line of Tim Jeffs Coloring Books and Lessons at TimJeffsArt.com • Etsy.com • Amazon.com

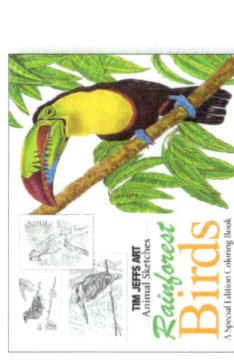
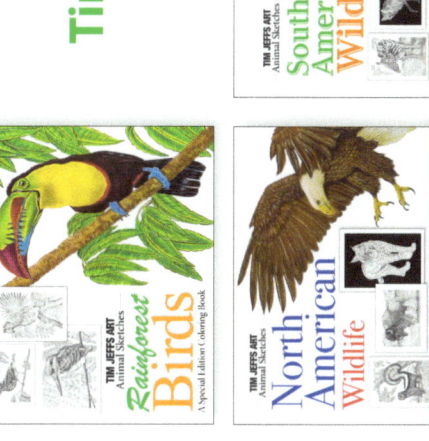
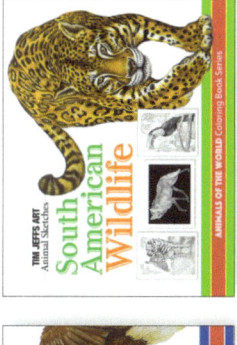
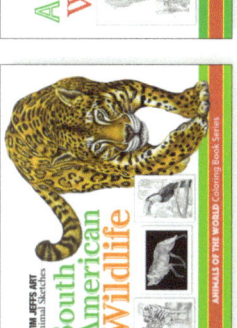
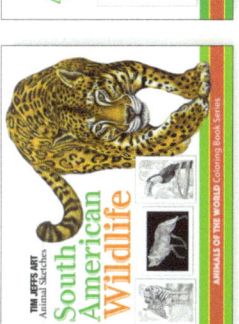
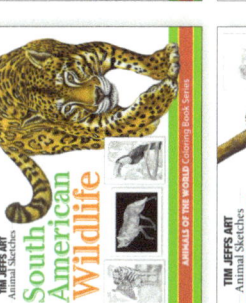
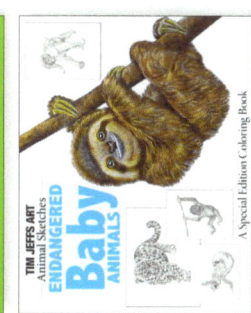
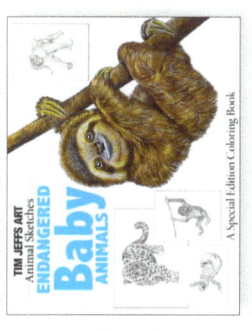
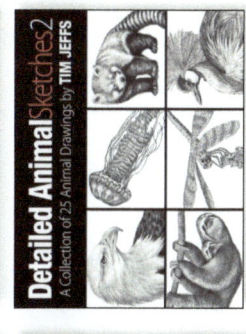
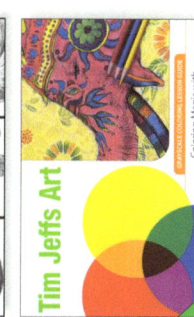
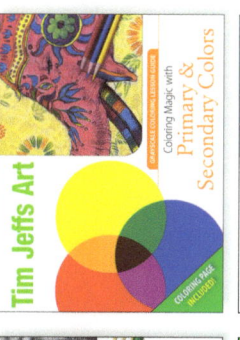
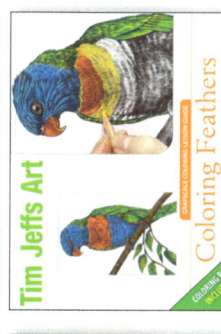
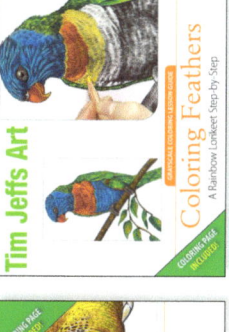
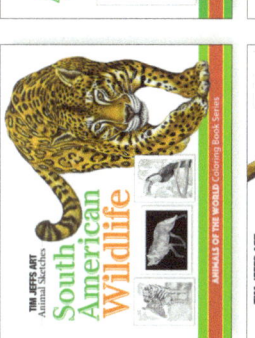
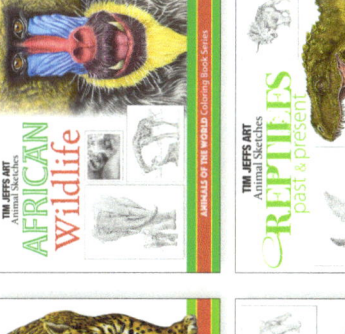
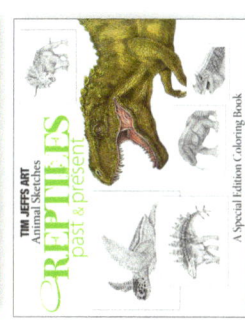
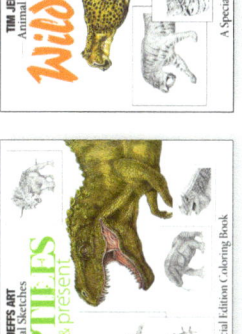
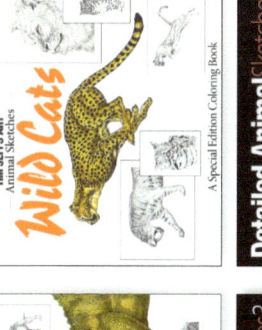
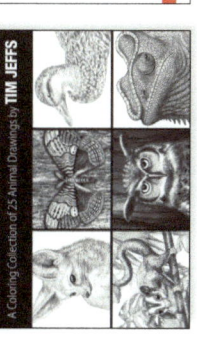
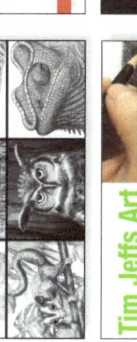
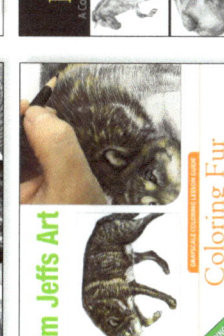
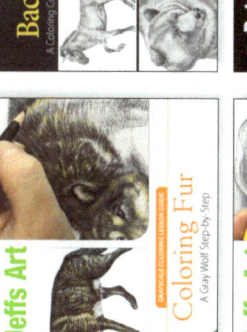
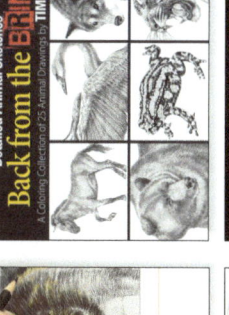
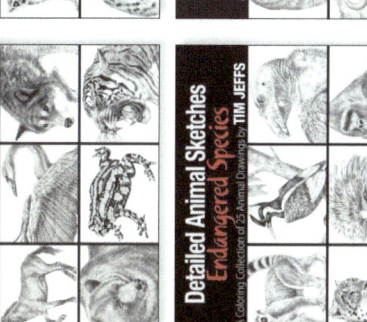
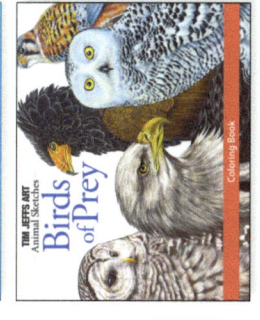
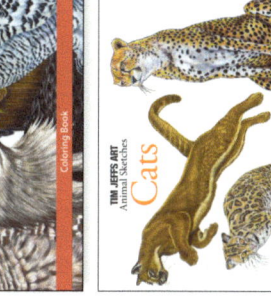
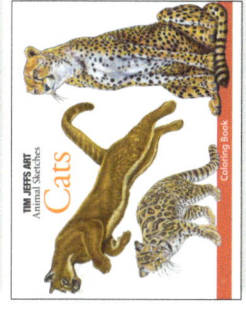
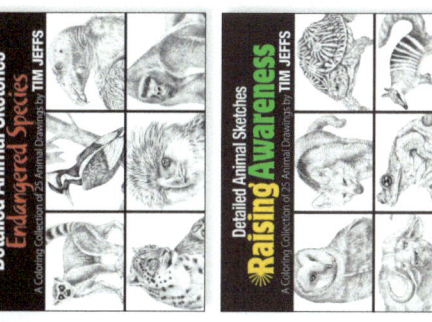
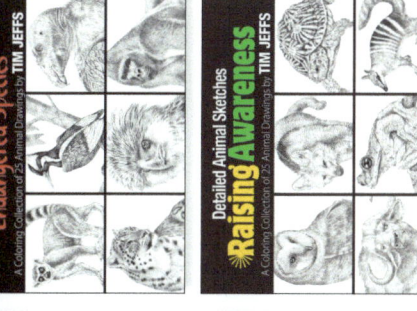
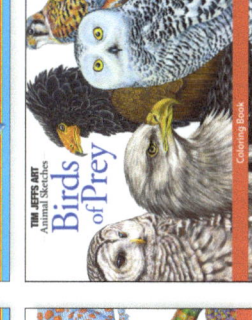
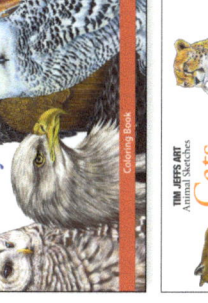
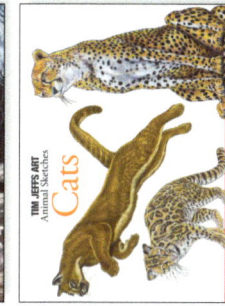

TIM JEFFS ART Online Resources

Share Your Creativity with the World!

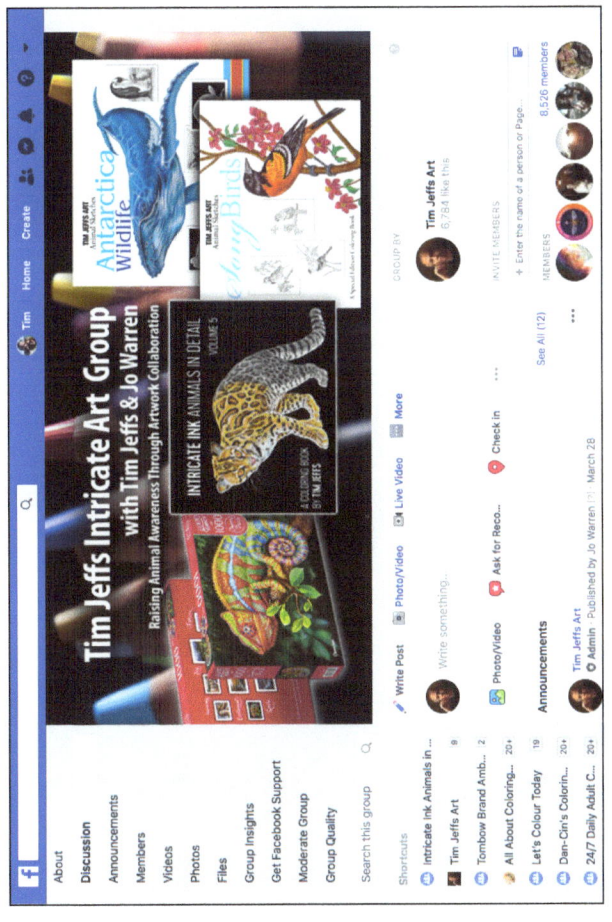

Join the ever-expanding coloring group of animal lovers who inspire each other through their colorings of the animals from Tim's books and lessons. With thousands of members from all around the world, Tim's Facebook group "Intricate Ink Coloring Group" is a creative and safe space where everyone is welcome. Jo Warren, the groups all-inspiring administrator will welcome you in with open arms and is there to encourage everyone to just have fun no matter your coloring skill level. Come join, we can't wait to have you as a member! Join Tim's Facebook Coloring Group at:

www.facebook.com/groups/intricateink

Visit the Home of Tim Jeffs Art

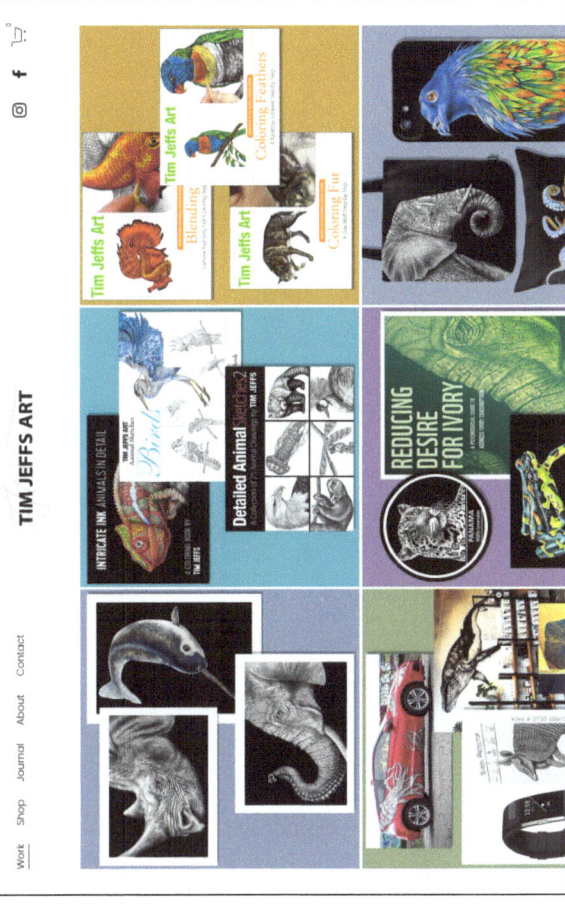

TimJeffsArt.com is my home on the web where I display all of my work and various projects. I hope you can stop by for a visit! You'll find my new shop where signed and unsigned prints of all of my animal drawings are available to purchase, along with the complete library of my digital download coloring books and grayscale coloring lessons. In the conservation section, you can see the projects that I am very proud of. Using my art to preserve wildlife is so important to me.

www.TimJeffsArt.com

www.ingramcontent.com/pod-product-compliance
Lightning Source LLC
Chambersburg PA
CBHW051220220526

45473CB00003B/1113